D1373710

MOTORMANiA

OFF-ROAD VEHICLES

Written by
PENNY WORMS

A⁺
Smart Apple Media

Published by Smart Apple Media,
an imprint of Black Rabbit Books
P.O. Box 3263, Mankato, Minnesota 56002
www.smartapplemedia.com

U.S. publication copyright © 2016 Smart Apple Media.
All rights reserved. International copyright reserved in
all countries. No part of this book may be reproduced in
any form without written permission from the publisher.

Published by arrangement with Watts Publishing, London.

Cataloging-in-Publication Data is available from the
Library of Congress
ISBN: 978-1-59920-995-1   (library binding)
ISBN: 978-1-68071-008-3   (eBook)

The author would like to thank Felix Wills and the
following for their kind help and permission to use
images: Jeremy Davey from the Thrust team; Dave
Rowley from the Bloodhound team; and the media
teams at Audi, BMW and McLaren.

Thanks to Felix Wills, Simon Belton at Yamaha Motor
(UK) Ltd, Mark Nevils at Polaris Industries, Urs Eiselin
at Sand-X and Ross Walker at KTM.

Picture Credits
007 MAGAZINE ARCHIVE/EON PRODUCTIONS: 27
bottom (from *The Spy Who Loved Me* © 1977 Danjaq
LLC and United Artists Corporation. All rights reserved.)
AFP/Getty Images: 16/17 background. James Cheadle /
Alamy: 15 bottom. King Features Syndicate, Inc: 15
center. KTM-Sportmotorcycle AG: 24/25 all images. Land
Rover: 18/19 background, 18 right. Mitsubishi Motors
Corporation: 20 center, 20 bottom. National Geographic/
Getty Images: 23 bottom. Polaris Industries, Inc: 10/11 all
images. Sand-X Motors: 12/13 all images. Shutterstock: 6/7
all images, 14, 18 bottom, 20/1 background, 26, 27 center.
Transtock Inc/Alamy: 23 centre.www.carphoto.co.uk: 17
right, 22. Yamaha Group: 8/9 all images.

Printed in the United States by CG Book Printers
North Mankato, Minnesota

Every attempt has been made to clear copyright.
Should there be any inadvertent omission,
please apply to the publisher for rectification.

Disclaimer: Some of the "Stats and Facts" are
approximations. Others are correct at time of writing,
but will probably change.

PO 1728
3-2015

CONTENTS

OFF-ROAD VEHICLES

Off-road vehicles are powerful and **nimble**. They can climb and scramble up hills, and drive through deep ditches or water without damage. Their large wheels or powerful **tracks** can cope with tough **terrain**. They can be fun to drive, too, because whatever nature throws at them, little slows them down.

GAS GUZZLERS

Big off-road vehicles need large, powerful engines that burn a lot of fuel. Many run on diesel fuel because diesel engines are less likely to break down than gasoline engines, which is not something you want to do in the middle of nowhere.

4X4

Most off-road vehicles have **four-wheel drive** (known as 4x4), which means the engine drives all four wheels at once. So, if one wheel gets stuck, the other wheels will still turn to get the vehicle out of trouble. Most car engines only drive the front or back wheels.

ACCESS ALL AREAS

There are some places where there are no roads or the roads are not surfaced properly. Rain can turn these tracks into mud. Also, heavy snowfall in some cold places can make roads icy and impassable to normal cars. Off-road vehicles are vital for the people living and working in these places.

ALL-TERRAIN VEHICLE (ATV)

Light and powerful, the all-terrain vehicle (ATV) is used by people who work outdoors and by those who enjoy outdoor activities. They are also ridden for fun and for sport. ATV racing is fast, thrilling, and dangerous.

FARMER FUN

The ATV is the farmer's friend. It can power across muddy fields and dusty ground with the speed of a motorbike, but is more comfortable and stable. ATVs are easy to drive and strong enough to pull a trailer. Farmers even use them for rounding up sheep.

SUPER SUSPENSION

shock arm
absorber

Most ATVs have an "independent **suspension.**" This means that the wheels are joined to the body of the vehicle by separate arms. So if one wheel goes over a rock, it doesn't affect the other wheels or cause the vehicle to tip. **Shock absorbers** soak up the bumps, too, to save the rider from a sore bottom!

STATS AND FACTS

- **Vehicle:** Yamaha YFZ450R
- **Top speed:** over 75 mph (120 km/h)
- **Country of origin:** Japan
- **Cost:** $9,000
- **Claim to fame:** A motocross-winning ATV that you can buy **race-ready**.

RACING QUADS

This Yamaha YFZ450R looks like a Transformer but it is actually one of the best racing ATVs. Powerful, lightweight, and tough, it is most at home on a **motocross** track, racing other ATVs at high speed.

SNOWMOBILE

Snowmobiles are a vital form of transport in parts of the world where snow is on the ground for a lot of the year. Instead of wheels, they have skis at the front and tracks at the back. The skis steer the snowmobile, while the tracks grip the snow.

SNOW RIDING

The Polaris 600 Rush is a snowmobile built for fun and sport. The Rush is light, agile, and powerful. It has a front and rear suspension, so it can speed over uneven snow and land smoothly and safely.

STATS AND FACTS

- **Vehicle:** Polaris 600 Rush
- **Top speed:** over 100 mph (160 km/h)
- **Cost:** from $11,000
- **Country of origin:** United States
- **Claim to fame:** It has a unique and advanced rear suspension.

COMFORT TOURING

The Polaris 600 IQ Touring is a snowmobile built for those wanting to travel in comfort. They are heavy and stable, with padded seats and larger fuel tanks. Touring snowmobiles can usually seat one or two people and they have a useful **reverse gear**.

ROLLING TRACK

rear suspension

track

The flat, rubber-like tracks have raised, molded "lugs" that act like cleats on football shoes. They dig into the snow to give the snowmobile **traction** or grip. The tracks go round and round, from front to back, pushing the snowmobile forward.

SAND-X

The Sand-X is a tracked all-terrain vehicle that is an ATV and snowmobile rolled into one. It has two front wheels and a single track at the back. It is mostly a fun vehicle for those living in the desert countries of the Middle East, where sand dunes are plentiful. It is capable of 114 mph (185 km/h) and has such amazing grip that it can do 0–60 in 2.8 seconds!

DUNE BUGGY

The Sand-X is more stable than a normal ATV because it sits very low to the ground and the front wheels are far apart. This means it is not as likely to tip over, and is safe even when powering over steep sand dunes.

- **Vehicle:** Sand-X
- **Top speed:** 114 mph (185 km/h)
- **Country of origin:** United Arab Emirates
- **Cost:** $24,000
- **Claim to fame:** The Sand-X can do 0–60 faster than a Ferrari Enzo!

ALL-TERRAIN

The Sand-X can travel on **gravel**, mud, and snow, but performs best on sand. It can carry 661 pounds (300 kg) of equipment and its large fuel tank means it can travel over 217 miles (350 km) before needing fuel. That's important when you're in the middle of a desert!

MISSION IMPOSSIBLE

The Sand-X has serious uses, too. It can be used by **border patrols** and search-and-rescue missions in the desert. There is also an armored version with a gun mounted by the handlebars.

JEEP

Jeep is the oldest name in off-road vehicles. It made its first appearance during World War II (1939–45) as part of the U.S. Army fleet. A war reporter at the time called it "as faithful as a dog, as strong as a mule, and as agile as a goat."

WILLY'S-OVERLAND

With the war raging in Europe, the U.S. Army put a challenge out to car makers to produce a 4x4 vehicle fit for war. Willy's-Overland beat Ford with their vehicle, which later became known as the Jeep.

- **Vehicle:** Jeep Wrangler 2.8 CRD Sport
- **Top speed:** 107 mph (172 km/h)
- **Country of origin:** United States of America
- **Cost:** from $28,000
- **Claim to fame:** A descendant of the oldest and most popular off-road vehicles ever.

EUGENE THE JEEP

The name "Jeep" seems to have come from Eugene the Jeep, a Popeye cartoon character. Eugene has the ability to appear and disappear, going anywhere he wants to, just like the Jeep. The less interesting story is that the name came from G.P., or "General Purpose," vehicle.

FUN IN THE SUN

Jeeps have now been replaced by Humvees (see page 16) in the U.S. Army. However, the Jeep Wrangler has become a popular road and off-road vehicle, especially in the United States. They have soft tops and doors that can be taken off for the ultimate open-air driving.

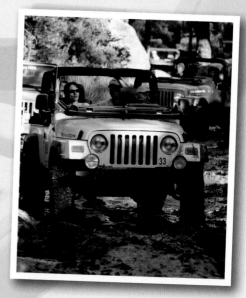

HUMVEE

The High Mobility Multipurpose Wheeled Vehicle, or the Humvee as it is known, is a four-wheel-drive vehicle used by the U.S. Army and other armies around the world. It can drive over deserts, across rocky ground, and through jungles safely and for long periods of time without stopping. It is a beast of a vehicle with a great many uses.

CLIMBING AND SWIMMING

A Humvee can climb up a 60-degree slope and can drive at a 40-degree sideways angle. It can go through water up to 4.9 ft (1.5 m) deep. It can tow and haul heavy loads. What it cannot do is go any more than 20 miles on 1 gallon of fuel (8.5km per liter)!

MULTI-PURPOSE

The Humvee is adapted for many uses—as a troop and equipment carrier, an ambulance, even as a missile launcher. However, the basic vehicles are the same. This is of great benefit to the mechanics who need to keep them in working order.

STATS AND FACTS

- **Vehicle:** Humvee M1151A1 w/B1
- **Top speed:** 70 mph (113 km/h) unarmoured
- **Country of origin:** United States
- **Cost:** $57,000 unarmored
- **Claim to fame:** A military vehicle so successful that it is now used by armies all over the world.

THE HUMMER

Hummers are road-going versions of the Humvee. They have the same basic technology. The tires can **deflate** and **inflate** at the touch of a button when driving. This is useful when driving on mud because flatter tires have more traction.

UTILITY VEHICLE

L and Rover is one of the most famous names in off-road vehicles, and the Defender is the brute of the pack. Comfort is low down on its list of qualities, as is speed. It makes it from 0–60 in an unimpressive 14.7 seconds. But it can climb a hill, wade through water, and pull a heavy trailer without breaking into a sweat.

ARMY SURPLUS

The Defender first appeared in 1948, just after World War II. It was the first non-military utility vehicle but was painted army green because the paint was cheap and plentiful. The body was made from **aluminium** because steel was in short supply.

INDESTRUCTIBLE

Many Defenders went to Africa, Asia, and Australia—anywhere where they needed tough cars to cope with bad roads. Over 60 years later, it is said that three out of four Defenders are still running. They are so solid and simply built that it is hard to destroy them. Also, aluminium doesn't rust like steel.

- **Vehicles:** Land Rover Defender
- **Top speed:** 82 mph (132 km/h)
- **Country of origin:** Great Britain
- **Cost:** from $28,000
- **Claim to fame:** An off-road classic with over 60 years of service.

PICK A STYLE

The new Defender is still a favorite with farmers, explorers, scientists, and park rangers—people who need a vehicle that can go anywhere and won't let them down. They can choose different styles, depending on whether they need to carry equipment or people or both.

SPORT UTILITY VEHICLE

The Mitsubishi Pajero is a sports utility vehicle or SUV. It is also known as the Montero or Shogun, depending on the country you live in. Like other SUVs, over time the Pajero has been made more powerful, more refined, and more comfortable.

OFF-ROAD

The Pajero has serious off-road **technology**. It has a safety system that controls how the car brakes and the way it grips the ground. There is also a large display telling drivers where they are and at what angle they are driving.

ON-ROAD

The Pajero has been through many changes to make it more city- and road-friendly. It now appeals to families just as much as the serious off-roader because it is roomy and comfortable inside.

STATS AND FACTS

- **Vehicle:** Mitsubishi Pajero 3.2 Diamond
- **Top speed:** 110 mph (177 km/h)
- **Country of origin:** Japan
- **Cost:** from $48,000
- **Claim to fame:** The most successful car ever in the Dakar Rally.

THE DAKAR RALLY

The Pajero is the most successful vehicle ever in the Dakar Rally, a 6,200 miles (10,000 km) endurance race. Originally the race went from Paris, France to Dakar in Northern Africa, but in 2008 it moved to South America. The competitors drive all sorts of vehicles, but they must make it across deserts, mountains, and extreme terrain.

OFF-ROAD RACERS

There are many off-road races around the world. The Dakar Rally is the most famous, but wherever there is an off-road challenge, there are enthusiasts who will build machines to tackle it. Often, they are made using the best parts from different vehicles.

BOWLER NEMESIS

The Nemesis is as tough as a car can get. Part Land Rover but with all-Bowler suspension and **chassis**, it can tackle all terrain with aggression, agility, and speed. If a tire gets damaged, the Nemesis has a built-in jack to raise all four wheels off the ground so the tire can be changed easily. And the tires are about the only thing on this mighty machine that can get damaged!

STATS AND FACTS

- **Vehicle:** Bowler Nemesis
- **Top speed:** 150 mph (241.4 km/h)
- **Country of origin:** UK
- **Cost:** from $180,000
- **Claim to fame:** Bowler are Dakar **veterans**, first with the Bowler WildCat and now with the Nemesis.

WACKY RACERS

In North America, there are many off-road races, such as the Best in the Desert series and the Baja 1000. These races attract the real wacky racers—some of the meanest and weirdest-looking machines around.

BAJA BUG

The **iconic** Volkswagen Beetle is now a classic car, loved by many. To see one ripping across the desert, sometimes with tires the size of a truck's, is a crazy but common sight in the Baja 1000. They are known as Baja Bugs.

DIRTBIKE

Off-road motorbikes are built mostly for racing. Some models are legal on the road, but it's on the dirt where they are really at home. And because they are so light, agile, and powerful, they are the kings of any off-road track—going faster than any other vehicle over the steep slopes, hard bumps, and tight turns.

KTM 50 SX

KTM are one of the best makers of off-road bikes. They produce bikes for every class of off-road race. The 50 SX is the smallest bike they make. It is used in junior motocross, where competitors can be as young as five years old.

- **Vehicle:** KTM 50 SX
- **Top speed:** not known
- **Country of origin:** Austria
- **Cost:** $4,000
- **Claim to fame:** The 2014 Junior 85cc Motocross World Champion was riding a KTM.

CLIMB AND CONQUER

Motocross is cross-country racing on specially built tracks. The bikes have knobby tires that grip the track so they can scramble up slopes. They also have super suspensions for a smoother ride.

ENDURANCE

KTM also builds bikes for long-distance enduro races. Enduro is like a car rally, with different stages on a variety of tracks. The engines are quieter and smoother than motocross engines. The bikes are also more comfortable for longer periods in the saddle.

AMPHIBIOUS VEHICLE

An amphibious vehicle is a road-going vehicle that can drive right into a sea or river and float and move like a boat. The most famous is "The Duck." Ducks are army vehicles that have been transformed into tour boat-buses in some of the world's biggest cities.

TAKE A TOUR

The name of the Duck came from its army name, the DUKW. They were first built for the U.S. Army to carry troops and weapons from ships to land during World War II. Many have been adapted to offer tourist trips around cities, like the one above in Boston. They drive around the city, and then take the tour right into the water.

STATS AND FACTS

- **Vehicle** DUKW (converted)
- **Top speed:** Land/Water 50/06 mph (80/10 km/h)
- **Cost:** $180,000 (to convert from a military vehicle)
- **Country of origin:** United States
- **Claim to fame:** DUKWs were used in the **D-Day landings**, transporting 160,000 troops to France!

WHY DOESN'T IT SINK?

The Duck has a watertight **hull**, a **propeller** and a **rudder**, just like a boat. The truck's engine powers a spinning propeller, which creates a force strong enough to move the heavy truck through the water.

UNDERWATER BOND

Probably the most famous amphibious vehicle ever is James Bond's Lotus Esprit in the film *The Spy Who Loved Me* (1977). The Lotus plunged into the water, sprouted fins and a propeller, and transformed into a submarine!

GLOSSARY

aluminium a lightweight metal that resists rust

border patrols police and other officials watch over their country's borders to stop people coming in illegally

chassis the metal frame on to which the wheels and body of the car are fixed

deflate to let air out of the tires

D-Day landings when British, American, and Canadian forces crossed the English Channel in boats in June 1944 and landed on the beaches of Nazi-occupied France

four-wheel drive when the engine of a vehicle powers all four wheels at once, rather than just two as on most cars

gravel a type of material used to surface roads

hull the main body of a boat that goes in the water

iconic something that, over time, has become an icon or symbol

inflate to fill up or pump up the tires with air

motocross cross-country motor racing on specially built dirt tracks

propeller a circle of blades, like a fan, that is spun round by a motor to propel or push a boat through water

race-ready when a vehicle can be bought and raced immediately, without having to be adapted or strengthened

reverse gear the gear on a vehicle that makes it go backward

rudder an underwater paddle that is used to steer a boat

shock absorbers air- or oil-filled parts that soak up bumps in the road

suspension a system of springs and shock absorbers that work between a vehicle and its wheels to absorb all the bumps in the ground

technology the use of science and the latest equipment

terrain what the ground is like, e.g. rocky, smooth, flat, or hilly

tracks a revolving metal or rubber band that drives a vehicle such as on a snowmobile

traction the way a vehicle's wheels grip the ground so it can drive the vehicle forward

veterans people or vehicles that have seen lengthy and active service

INDEX